# A KID'S GUIDE TO FEELING

# FEELING EXCITED

## BY KIRSTY HOLMES

# BookLife PUBLISHING

©2018
BookLife Publishing
King's Lynn
Norfolk PE30 4LS

**ISBN:** 978–1–78637–271–0

All facts, statistics, web addresses and URLs in this book were verified as valid and accurate at time of writing. No responsibility for any changes to external websites or references can be accepted by either the author or publisher.

**Written by:**
Kirsty Holmes

**Edited by:**
Holly Duhig

**Designed by:**
Danielle Rippengill

## Image Credits

All images are courtesy of Shutterstock.com, unless otherwise specified. With thanks to Getty Images, Thinkstock Photo and iStockphoto. Front Cover – MarinaMay, yayasya, jirawat phueksriphan, Piotr Urakau, VaLiza, Gelpi, maxim ibragimov. Images used on every page – MarinaMay, yayasya, Piotr Urakau. 5 & 6 – T–Kot. 6 – Rvector. 8 – 3445128471, x4wiz, Sergieiev, Riccardo Mayer. 9 – VaLiza, Dean Drobot, Rawpixel.com. 11 – Jacek Chabraszewski, Jacek Chabraszewski, Mark Nazh. 12 – maxim ibragimov, Cultura Motion. 12 & 13 – Evellean. 14 – gst, yitewang, Melody A, Oleksandr Malysh. 15 – Eva Foreman, Ruslan Guzov, Dean Drobot. 16 – SofiaV. 17 – Ilike. 18 – Kovalchuk Oleksandr. 21 – CebotariN, Africa Studio, PastelStone, Daxiao Productions.

# CONTENTS

Words that look like **this** can be found in the glossary on page 24.

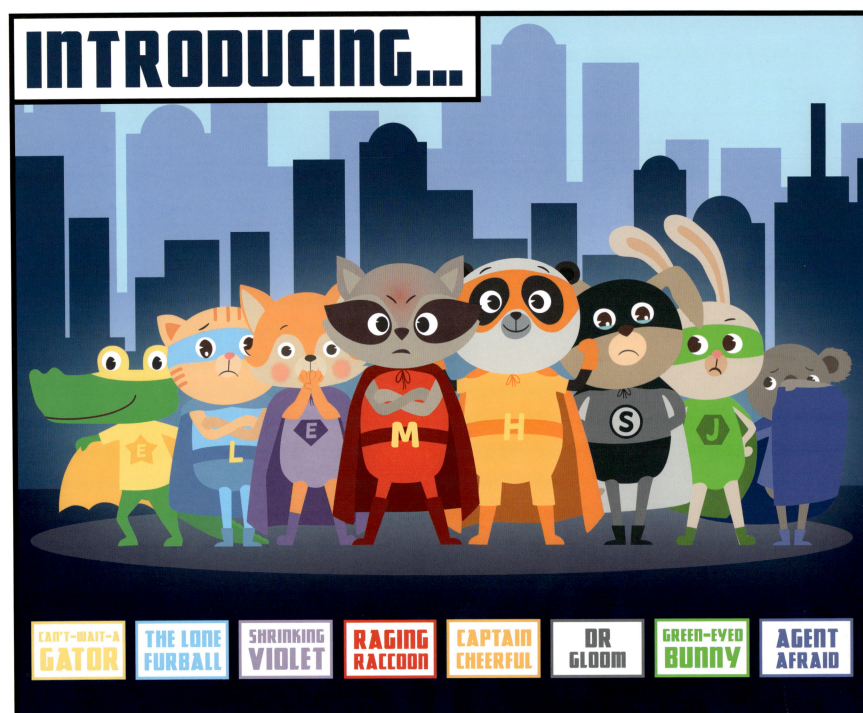

# INTRODUCING...

| CAN'T-WAIT-A GATOR | THE LONE FURBALL | SHRINKING VIOLET | RAGING RACCOON | CAPTAIN CHEERFUL | DR GLOOM | GREEN-EYED BUNNY | AGENT AFRAID |

# AGENTS OF F.E.E.L.S!

## FEELING.EVERY.EMOTION.LIKE.SUPERHEROES!

We all have **emotions**, or feelings, all the time. Our feelings are very important. They help us think about the world around us, and know how we want to **react**.

Sometimes, we feel good. Other times, we feel bad.

Everyone is cheering! Our hero is feeling really excited.

# HOW DO WE FEEL WHEN WE'RE EXCITED?

You might feel a **swell** in your chest…

…you might feel a rush of energy…

…or get **goosebumps**…

…and you might feel **tingly** and nice.

You might feel like you want to shout…

Being excited feels really good!

…or laugh out loud…

…or jump and dance around.

9

# HOW DO WE LOOK WHEN WE'RE EXCITED?

# WHY DO WE FEEL EXCITED?

FEELING EXCITED IS AN IMPORTANT EMOTION.

Life can be a bit boring sometimes.

Human beings like to get rewards.

MEDAL!

CAKE!

MONEY!

We can feel excited about these.

12

# THINGS THAT MAKE US EXCITED

NEW EXPERIENCES!

PARTIES!

THE FUTURE!

You might feel excited if you get something new…

…or if you are going to see someone you love.

We can feel excited about special **events**.

# WHEN FEELING EXCITED IS GOOD

Feeling excited can be a good thing. If you are looking forward to something cool, you can begin to enjoy it, even before it happens.

# WHEN FEELING EXCITED IS BAD

Sometimes, it's just not the right time to show we are excited.

If our feelings of excitement get out of control, they can stop feeling good, and start feeling bad. This is called feeling 'overwhelmed'.

It's not nice to feel too excited.

19

# DEALING WITH FEELINGS

Can't-Wait-A-Gator is a little too excited.

Her friends will help her to feel calmer. Agents of F.E.E.L.S: GO!

# LET'S HELP!

Talking about your feelings can help you to understand why you feel excited.

# GLOSSARY

**BODY LANGUAGE** — things a person does with their body that tell you how they feel

**EMOTIONS** — a strong feeling such as joy, hatred, sorrow, or fear

**EVENTS** — special occasions

**GOOSEBUMPS** — little bumps on the skin caused by cold or excitement

**MOTIVATED** — feeling like you want to do something

**REACT** — act or respond to something that has been done

**REWARDS** — something promised as a treat, for effort

**SWELL** — grow larger or expand

**TINGLY** — prickly feeling in the skin

# INDEX